Poems
for
Princesses
with
Peas
Under
Their
Mattresses

Poems for Princesses with Peas Under Their Mattresses

Maithy Vu

**Poems for Princesses with Peas
Under Their Mattresses**

Copyright © 2024 by Maithy Vu
All rights reserved.

First edition April 2024

Text edited by Aubrie Goslin and Cleo Miele
Cover design by Zakarius Fariury
Interior image by Maithy Vu

ISBN: 978-0-9963822-7-4 (paperback)
ISBN: 978-0-9963822-4-3 (eBook)

www.maithyvu.com

Dear Reader,

Once upon a time, you were told captivating myths, fables, and fairytales by grown-ups you trusted. Perhaps, like me, you believed the words that were handed down to you.

Then, you got older, and those stories began to lose value in a life more complicated. You began to wonder whether the morals you'd learned still held meaning for the person you had become.

This poetry collection is the delicate product of my efforts to make sense of the connection between the girl I once was and the woman I am. The tales I consumed became tools for the knots I spent restless nights unraveling. Some, I had to cut apart in order to find peace. They became lullabies I sang to myself.

I hope these verses reignite the princess in you—the one who still believes in goodness and courage and magic. I hope they serve as your armor when you must face the monsters of youth and the dragons of adulthood.

Most of all, I hope they help you sleep.

Ever after,
Maithy

i.

You're just a fairytale, they say.
Your name never spoken as
an emblem of Strength, Drive, or Wit—
as though it doesn't take strength
to stay kind despite others' cruelty,
or drive to understand
how work comes before play.
It was only when Prince Charming
was the last thing on your mind
that he called after you.
And as far as wit, they should know
when shoes fit, they don't fall off
unless their owners want them to.

ii.

You are a well of tenderness—
buckets overflowing with mercy
until your depths run dry.
They mine seven sides of you,
picking them apart
to find diamonds
until you no longer trust
what mirrors reflect.
And what is left of you
is taken by princes who
take without asking—
their pristine white horses
stomping on your nature
until it's cold as snow.
Little dove, remember:
when they want
a bite of your apple,
do not be afraid
to give them a taste
of your poison.

iii.

my arms cannot reach men who stand
so i crawl beneath their clawing hands
i drag along their games so wicked
creep around their words so twisted
inch my way between parasites
grasping for any sign of flight
my arms cannot reach men who stand
so i crawl beneath their clawing hands

iv.

i was told i had child-bearing hips at age thirteen.

street calls came every quarter moon, and i learned
to hide the swells of the cobblestones that made up
my shelter.

the stones, stacked so high, became a tower no
stableboy nor lord could climb.

each remark toward my body became a strand of
the braid that weighed me down until i could not
recall its language.

my reluctance gave me the stain of a sorceress;
the maiden in me began to like being feared.

so the next time they told me to let down my hair,
i grabbed the sharpest pair of shears i owned.

v.

I graze the surface without a voice, observing how they stand on staghorn branches to enhance their stature.

They float upon a strip of land soaked red as though their reverence bleeds with every step.

Kelp of blues, pinks, purples wrap around them, a ballet of jellyfish emitting their own spotlights.

Flashes burst as they perform their stillness. "Over here!" cry the land anglerfish. "Look this way!"

Their egos beg to be praised, ogled, idolized so they can rest easy on the pillows stuffed with the feathers of my friends.

*

I picture myself beside them, having learned to walk with a confidence that only comes from years of being knocked down.

The buzz beckons me to be a part of the world where the sun burns my face—

to dance upon hardened sand and join their feasts upon round-cut wood they pretend didn't come from shipwrecks—but I can't seem to let go of the deep.

vi.

They liked me when I did my duty
with a floating smile
so I ate a mushroom to make myself smaller
until I ran out of bandwidth
trying to catch up to
white rabbits
I spiraled
circling back endlessly
to a caterpillar in charge who
gaslit me by blowing smoke rings
filled with excuses
and the others threw me a tea party
to keep my mind out of the hole
I was falling into
and when I negotiated with the Queen of Hearts
for a better hand
I learned she wears them on her sleeve
because she has none
inside her chest
So I ate the bread we broke
to make myself grow
hoping they would see me
for all I am
only for them to say
"You're too big for us."

vii.

She's got all her ducks in a row.

She gives them names like Reliability, Creativity, and Determination.

She tells them that they're siblings and makes them take turns doing the chores.

Another named Genius visits like a family friend who eats their food and joins weekend vacations.

They take group portraits in matching yellow fuzz with their beaks wide open.

Lately, an ugliness has developed in the darkroom.

The ducks know it doesn't belong, but they're too scared to address it.

They all keep low quacks and hope the ugly turns into something else later on.

viii.

They warn me to stay away
from your glazed stories
and chocolate-covered lies—
that indulging in the sweet nothings
will cause a toothache so inflamed,
it will never heal.

Though I know the path
home will lead to fire,
the blood that binds us
throbs within my fingertips,
and I can't help but pick up
the crumbs you leave me.

ix.

I slept for a hundred years.

They declared it laziness.

No one bothered to ask why I hexed myself unconscious, no one checked my hands to see if I'd pricked my finger on a spindle in a haystack. No one carried my body to a fairy to determine what institutional curse rendered me frozen. Rather, they hid me from the villagers so no one would see the disappointment their lady had become and shook me until I lived half awake, forgetting the dream I once laid upon.

x.

Loneliness is a cage.
It is the numbness you feel when you start listing
names in your head of people you could call,
trying to determine who would understand even
an inkling of what's inside you, only to realize you
don't want to disturb their crickets, and you'd
rather not tarnish the reputation you pulled
strings for, so you let the whale swallow you until
you decide nothing's real and do your best to avoid
puddles, not wanting to catch a glimpse
as your nose grows.

xi.

queens give their crowns to fools
just to make them kings
then the kings leave their lovers
when they realize they want queens

xii.

I met a boy when we were young.
He taught me how to fly over
the shadows that followed us
when all we fought were pirates
who wanted the treasures we hunted.

I met a boy when we were young.
He saved me from falling and drowning
into the depths of adulthood
until I could walk the plank
without being afraid of what lay below.

I met a boy when we were young.
He took life so unseriously,
I could never tell when the dust
he sprinkled over me held magic
and when it didn't.

I met a boy when we were young.
Then I grew up,
and he refused to do the same.

xiii.

I kissed a frog that tasted like
watermelon in autumn

I kissed a frog that shielded me from its venom

I kissed a frog that hopped on
lily pads under thunderstorms

I kissed a frog that promised to transform

I kissed a frog that warned me
how many flies it trapped with its tongue

I kissed a frog that croaked smoke from its lungs

I kissed a frog that swore
I would love it until the end

I kissed a frog and never sought a prince again

xiv.

They call it a syndrome, as though I have no will when it comes to staying in a castle where the objects in it are livelier than the people.

I scan the library of your moods in hopes of figuring out which to read, but the walls are covered with old tales and times I don't understand.

The distance between our souls feels longer than the table where we have our silent suppers.

We fight over which one of us is the beast, only to learn we were both broken by a spell.

I'm merely a guest of your heart—inventing ways to get you to love me again

before the last petal falls.

xv.

in a land where unpleasant creatures roamed
a land of violence, acid, and foam
where one could perish for being tame
and monsters fought each other for game
lived a girl so very frightened
for nothing felt quite right, and so
she kept to herself as much as she could
until she forced herself to face the woods
she felt it was her time to grow
by living things she did not know
but her stroll was not a tranquil one
and the daunting path had barely begun
when she heard a sound! a sound!
and as she turned around, around
oh, she did not expect
a troll breathing down her neck!

*

it roared and growled and slashed and howled,
taking her in the palm of its hand
she screamed, unbowed, "ogre, put me down!"
but when she looked into its eyes, she saw a man—
the monster was not a monster at all
but as human as she in its rises and falls
not perfect, not treacherous either
just as weak and just as tired
just as lost, just as cold
with just as many stories untold
"what are you?" she asked. "monster or man?"
it said, "i'm like you, whatever i am."
so monster and monster, woman and man
walked through the woods, hand in hand

xvi.

I trudge through a race I never asked for.

The twenty-five-year-olds fast-walk through suited crowds with gold insurance plans that let them see a shrink.

I wonder if they know they'll grow tired of doing laps on tracks where they're replaceable.

Snapshots of their petite portions mock the rice bowl I've turned into three meals.

The world is full of hares earning carrots for carats that gleam beneath sunrays through glass ceilings.

Dad tells me to let him know when I need rent money.

Every night, I pray that I am a tortoise.

xvii.

Mother promised to trade me for a hundred knots, as if my worth were made up of pieces. Her world is of the rich and the poor; she neglects the graceless and the true. "Keep your back straight," she reminds me. "Don't chew so loudly." The suitors cut down bamboo like my agency. I long to be free from the roots invading the soil of our homeland. *Unstick. Unstick.*

xviii.

Grandmother forgot my name
She called me Red instead
Her skin's so gray, she looks
like a wolf in that bed

I wonder if she thinks my name is such
because it's the color of lì xì,
of luck, and ớt, and lanterns,
her pinches upon my cheeks

The three stripes on our flag,
the styrofoam trays of sticky rice
The incense on our altars
and the cross where she worked nights

*

What memories leave us
during the last of our days?
Do the bad ones fade?
Do the good ones stay?

I remember playful insults
and bills slipped into my hands
"What big thighs you have."
"Here, take a grand."

The clutter on her kitchen island—
baskets of dragon fruit and bread
Grandmother forgot my name
Instead, she called me Red

xix.

I'm
convinced
that I'm
supposed
to be
the one to pull the sword out
of the stone but I'm too
afraid
of the
attention
I'll get
when
they
learn
what
I've
done
so I
never
let
myself
take
the
grip
.

xx.

I found a lamp buried in sand, eroded from the rocks thrown at me.

First, I wished for Wealth, and the genie said, "You must earn it from the sultan."

So I turned each tear I wept into a jewel polished with time and sweat.

Second, I wished for Love, and the genie said, "You must leave after a thousand and one nights."

So I wove a carpet out of the threads we hung by and flew us over the sundial's silent chime.

Last, I wished for Respect, and the genie said, "Not all are destined for such."

So I set him free.

xxi.

You think your wealth lies in
numbers and well-known names,
but soon they'll see through
all your selfish claims
You'll find your little subjects
will someday break their loyalty,
while I live on in colored castles—
for kindness breathes royalty
Words shall be my currency,
friendships, my treasure
Go on, parade your possessions,
hunt your sheep for pleasure
Flaunt your lavish titles;
I drip with stories you'll never own
And should you seek forgiveness,
I'll have you bow before my throne

xxii.

Your heart bleeds green
with every step I take,
so you banish me for lacking
the thing he took away

You strip me of the beauty,
too much for you to bear,
but power is all you shed
upon the coils of my hair

For when they rip your body
as though it is theirs to own...
Nothing feels greater
than watching theirs turn to stone

So if this is your punishment,
may this curse be my bliss
And if you wish for my silence,
may this verse be my hiss

xxiii.

three centuries gone by
where you were crucified
casted spells made assault
your own foolish fault
they told your mouth to stop
said you'd burn the crops
whether you were old or young
had thirteen children or none
whether you walked short or tall
they sought to burn you all
my darlings! news break:
today they're at the stake
rise Rebecca, come forth Mary
'cause tonight we'll unbury
the souls that they sold
and the black lies that they told
we'll call 'em guilty if they float
justice if they drown
ashes, ashes
they all
fall
down

xxiv.

You cry when there is no wolf in sight, and

    I rush to your aid in case you see things
            the rest of us are blind to.

You cry when there is no wolf in sight, and

I remind myself that you are just a boy who was
           put in charge of an entire flock.

You cry when there is no wolf in sight, and

I build a fence of stability for the sheep you count
           when you can't sleep.

You cry when there is no wolf in sight, and

I sprint toward your howls with blistered feet,
wondering if there will ever be a day when I won't

           come running.

xxv.

The lark lives under a lion's rule
He expects her to sing whenever he pleases
The lark cries what melodies she can
"Am I enough? Am I enough?"

The lion's roar warns the wild
of the influence within his paws
Every creature bows to the ground
And the lark cries, "Am I enough?"

The lark is asked to build a nest
for the lion to rest his head
She gathers grassroots and horsefeathers
All the while, crying, "Is this enough?"

The lark wonders if there's a princess
who'd love to have her as a pet
Oh, wouldn't it be lovely?
Still, she cries, "I wouldn't be enough."

*

One day, the lark spots a magpie
soaring through a cloudless sky
with crooked beak and wounded wings
who believes in itself enough

So, when the lion falls asleep
on the nest that the lark did weep
She springs from the cave he trapped her in,
praying she'll be enough

And when the dove coos servility
And the raven laughs at others' expense
The lark decides
she has cried enough

xxvi.

They
    told
        me
            about
    the giant
            at the
                top of
                    the stalk—
                that I'll
            get sent
                up there
                if I earn
                    magic beans.
        They say   he can
            smell the
        blood of a
virtuous woman;
            he'll know if
        I am one as soon as
            I get there.
    I want to believe
                    his *fee-fi-fo-fum*,
        but every golden egg
        in my possession was
        shaped by my own hand.

xxvii.

I sat in a chair that creaked
from the weight of my labor
and gave me splinters every time I cared.
It buckled when I gambled on my dreams,
so I decided it was much too hard.

I sat in a chair with cushions that
swallowed my dreams into their fluff.
It rocked me to sleep until I forgot
about its stains,
and I thought it was much too soft.

I sat in a chair that urged me to stay put
until I spilled my colors onto the page.
My back grew sore from the wood, but my dreams
climbed their way up the legs, and I knew
that one was just right.

xxviii.

I built a house of straw that swayed with the wind
and, amidst the quakes, stayed tame.
They put a torch to its roof
and huffed to spread the flames.

I built a house of sticks that let the sunlight
stream glowing cracks along the floor.
They rolled a boulder down a hill
and watched it go crashing through the door.

I built a house of bricks that kept me warm during
winter and cool when they came knocking.
"Open up," they demanded. "Let us in."

Not by the hair of my chinny chin chin.

xxix.

The dragons paint your palace skies

                                 with black smoke

They expect you to coil when you're smothered in their hot breaths—expect you to kneel at the sight

                                 of the soldiers they send

They don't know how chainmail clings to your spirit, or how more chivalry lies in your finger than

                                 their entire order

For when they've taken your sword and slain your horse, your past becomes

                                 the knight in shining armor

And when they've burned down your house more times than you can count,

                                 you are no longer afraid of fire

xxx.

Rumpelstiltskin gives a different name whenever he's at the coffee shop. He'd rather not spell it for the barista who will cross it out and try again.

He repeats it when he introduces himself to those who will have to know him.

He spins the syllables into gold so they'll remember it, but doesn't correct them when they pronounce it wrong.

This little game never bothered him much.

He knows one day they won't have to guess it, for it'll be heard wherever they go.

xxxi.

i hold six hundred names in my head
of women who've fought
the injustices of their
so-called paths—
warriors with shields, leaders with promises,
women who broke down gates
built to keep them out.
their valor follows me wherever i lose strength—
commanding me to get up from the dirt
i've grown so used to.
i hold six hundred voices in my head
sighing at the mess of the battleground
that's caused me more wounds
than i have bandages for.
i hold six hundred faces in my head
of women trampled and lost,
who slept in trenches with
hope-filled hallucinations,
and i shall add my story as six-oh-one
by staring down loaded guns
until they're forced to write about me.

xxxii.

She sleeps in a matchbox under my pillow—
tall as a thumb, thin as a splinter.

Her curse is that she cares too much.
It opens her like a wound asking to be infected.

She orders me to evade the toads.
I capture the butterflies she makes her friends.

"I belong in a flower," she tells me. "Find me a
garden so I may frolic through its rich soil."

When I do, she meets a prince her size and weds
him on a zinnia in the dead of spring.

*

I think she'll leave me be, but she builds a house of matchsticks upon my shoulder.

"I deserve to have wings," she tells me. "Fashion me a pair so I may fly through temperate clouds."

"I am tired," I tell her. "And I don't have magical powers."

She stomps her foot on my collarbone.

"Yes, you do!" she pouts as I force her back into my pocket. "Yes, you d—"

xxxiii.

My heart may not be made of stone,

        but I rule the ground like it's my own

I stack my words into a throne,

        turn raging sandstorms into poems

The wastelands, I paint with rhythm—

        making of them my own faithful kingdom

And before the noble know what hits them,

        my verse becomes their new religion

My pen seeps water into desolate lines

        as I take gravel and fuse it with rhymes

Let the bones unearthed be signs of life

        These finds keep my sovereignty alive

www.ingramcontent.com/pod-product-compliance
Lightning Source LLC
Chambersburg PA
CBHW030458010526
44118CB00011B/1002